Environmental Awareness:
TOXIC WASTE

AUTHOR
By Mary Ellen Snodgrass

EDITED BY
Jody James, Editorial Consultant
Janet Wolanin, Environmental Consultant

DESIGNED AND ILLUSTRATED BY
Vista III Design, Inc.

BANCROFT-SAGE PUBLISHING, INC.
601 Elkcam Circle, Suite C-7, P.O. Box 355
Marco, Florida 33969-0355

Library of Congress Cataloging-in-Publication Data

Snodgrass, Mary Ellen.
 Environmental awareness—toxic waste / by Mary Ellen Snodgrass;
edited by Jody James, Editorial Consultant; Janet Wolanin,
Environmental Science Consultant; illustrated by Vista III Design.
 p. cm.—(Environmental awareness)
 Includes index.
 Summary: Discusses the causes of toxic waste and its effects on the
environment and life. Outlines methods of disposal and how to protect
yourself from toxic waste effects.
 ISBN 0-944280-27-7
 1. Hazardous wastes—Juvenile literature. 2. Hazardous wastes—
Management—Juvenile literature. [1. Hazardous wastes—
Environmental aspects.] I. James, Jody, Wolanin, Janet. II. Vista III
Design. III. Title. IV. Title: Toxic waste. V. Series: Snodgrass, Mary Ellen.
Environmental awareness.
TD1030.5.S66   1991
363.72'87—dc20

International Standard Book Number:	Library of Congress Catalog Card Number:
Library Binding 0-944280-27-7	91-7427
	CIP
	AC

PHOTO CREDITS
COVER: Minnesota PCA; Nancy Ferguson p. 38; J.E. Kirk p. 13, 15, 16, 41; K.G.
Melde p. 28; Minnesota PCA p. 9, 27, 32; Silver Image, Mark Barrett p. 22; Unicorn
Photography, Martha McBride p. 18, 36, 37; USAF p. 17; Vista III Design, Ginger
Gilderhus p. 4, 7, 35, Grant Gilderhus p. 10, 21, 23, 24, 34, 44, Jackie Larson p. 14.

TABLE OF CONTENTS

Without realizing it most people purchase products everyday that contain toxic wastes.

CHAPTER ONE

DANGEROUS WASTE

Everyday, people make shopping lists and drive to the supermarket, drugstore, or hardware store to buy the items they need. In addition to food and clothing, people need other products. They buy shoe and furniture polishes, nail polish remover, bleach, oven and toilet bowl cleaners, mothballs, insect sprays, rodent killer, paint, batteries, art and hobby supplies, and oil for squeaky bikes and doors. When these shoppers return home, they throw out their old, empty containers that once held similar products. Without realizing it, these people are discarding **toxic wastes**.

Toxic wastes are very dangerous materials that have been thrown away. They are more dangerous than food scraps, paper, cardboard, wood, plastic, or glass. The United States government has classified more than 400 materials as extremely dangerous. In addition, many new chemical substances have not yet been tested to see if they are toxic. These substances may someday also join the list of very dangerous materials.

Toxic waste can seriously damage the **environment** for many years. It may poison air, drinking water, or land. It can get into farm animals and vegetables and poison the people who eat them. As the human population grows, the amount of toxic waste increases. No one is safe from the dangers. People need to know more about toxic waste to keep themselves safe and healthy.

Ted Kilby and his parents had to move to a new location to avoid toxic waste. Read what they learned about toxic waste in their neighborhood.

MOVING DAY

With tears in his eyes, Ted Kilby looked out the living room window at the lawn. In the front yard stood a "FOR SALE" sign. A truck was backing up to the carport to begin loading the Kilby family's furniture. The living room was almost empty.

Ted could not concentrate on the sunny April morning or his cocker spaniel, Betsy, who was snapping at a bee near the juniper bushes. All he could see was the ugly sign. All he could think about was leaving Denton, his hometown.

"Now, Ted," Loretta Kilby said, "it won't be so bad. We'll find a neighborhood in another town that you will like as much as you like this one. Maybe even better. Just wait and see."

"Mom," Ted sighed, "I feel so sad. I'm going to miss everybody."

"I know, son," she replied. "I'll miss my friends, too, especially the Hendersons."

"Do we have to move? Are you and Dad sure that we have to go?" Ted looked hopefully at his mother. He wished that she would change her mind about moving from Denton.

Sometimes, people have to move to a new location to avoid toxic waste.

"Ted, the danger of living here is too great. Since Howco Chemical began burying barrels of toxic waste in this valley, the chance of someone getting a terrible illness has become a daily hazard. We can't take the risk that something might happen to you or your little brother," she concluded. "So we have to move."

"But, Mom," Ted continued, "if Russ and I stop playing near the old dump, if we never go near those dirty old rusty barrels, we won't get sick. We'll be more careful, I promise."

"I realize that you and Russ didn't mean to endanger yourselves last summer," his mother replied. "But nobody knew then that the barrels contained deadly wastes. It wasn't until the health department called in investigators from the **Environmental Protection Agency [EPA]** that we even heard about toxic wastes. We still don't know very much about them."

"Why would that company put dangerous stuff in our neighborhood?" Ted asked.

"It began years ago, maybe before the company knew that the wastes could cause sickness. There haven't been any new barrels at that site since you were a baby," she said.

"Well, maybe the stuff inside has rotted by now. Maybe it can't hurt anybody any more," Ted suggested.

"I'm sorry to dampen all your ideas, Ted, but toxic waste is not that simple. It doesn't just evaporate like a puddle of water. It doesn't decay like dead leaves. Once the land is **polluted**, nobody knows how far down the toxic waste may have spread," she replied.

"We may be using unsafe drinking water," she added. "We may be touching polluted soil or breathing polluted air. I can't take chances with my family." She patted Ted's back with a gentle hand and leaned her cheek against the top of his head. Then she began removing the curtains from the overhead window rod.

Ted propped his elbows on the window sill. He looked out at the lawn and across the street. Houses dotted the area for as far as he could see. It seemed impossible that all his friends and neighbors were in danger. How could a chemical company be so careless? Why didn't somebody stop them from dumping years ago? Why would anybody want to endanger innocent people with toxic waste?

Toxic waste stored in barrels is very dangerous. The Environmental Protection Agency investigates areas where barrels have been improperly dumped or stored.

9

Coal mines were often a source of dangerous wastes, poisoning people, plants and animals. Today the problem of manufactured waste has become more life-threatening than anything in nature.

CHAPTER TWO

SOURCES OF TOXIC WASTES

Ted has asked some difficult questions. Unfortunately, nobody has answers to all of them. Toxic wastes are not new. There have always been substances that can poison people, animals, and plants. Centuries ago, coal mines were a source of dangerous wastes. Even natural substances, such as strong alkali salts, make certain springs and creeks unfit for drinking.

But now the problem of manufactured wastes has become more life-threatening than anything in nature. More people populate the earth. Factories create more products to make human life easier. These factories also produce waste. Finding a place for the waste becomes a greater problem each day. **Landfills** can't handle it all.

Even more serious than household wastes are wastes from institutions and factories. Hospitals have soiled bandages and human tissue to dispose of. A large manufacturing plant can turn out more toxic waste in one day than a family can produce in a lifetime.

How can manufacturers safely dispose of all this waste? How can government officials assure people that the environment around them is safe? These and other questions help focus our attention on the problem of toxic waste.

PEOPLE AND SOLID WASTE

Making garbage cannot be stopped. Most products come in wrappers or containers. These unwanted wastes, along with old newspapers, leaves and twigs, broken appliances, worn-out clothing, and old toys, often end up in the garbage can. **Sanitation workers** remove the garbage from some neighborhoods in trash removal trucks. They haul it to a landfill and deposit it with the rest of the city's junk.

In other areas, waste removal is more complicated. People **recycle** much of their trash. They separate usable waste from unusable waste. They tear old cloth into usable rags. Objects such as glass bottles, newspapers, plastic containers, cardboard, and aluminum cans go into **recycling bins**. These products can be remade into usable goods. Newspaper can be ground up and reprocessed into new paper goods. Glass can be crushed and mixed with asphalt for paving roads. Aluminum cans, cardboard, glass, and plastic can be recycled and used again and again to hold soft drinks, juice, soap, or beauty products. Recycling reduces the amount of garbage that has to be disposed of.

Not all wastes are recyclable, however. For example, fruit juice containers made of a blend of plastic, paper, and aluminum foil cannot be separated into recyclable materials. Some types of unusable household waste is hazardous, even deadly. This waste is toxic to humans, animals, and plants.

Nearly 10% of all garbage is toxic. Every year the United States creates a ton of toxic waste for each citizen. These toxic substances come from many sources. Some are easily recognized, but some are less obvious.

These items can all be recycled.

People recycle much of their waste. They separate the usable items from the unusable items. New products can then be made from the reusable waste.

13

INDUSTRY AND TOXIC WASTE

Industry causes the most toxic waste. For example, when miners remove coal, copper, and other metals from the earth, they must separate usable ore from waste called **slag**. Many forms of slag are toxic.

Factories, too, create harmful **by-products**. Many factories, such as those that produce glues or rubber, use **solvents**. These strong chemicals help break down other substances during the manufacturing process. The fumes from some solvents are deadly, both to workers and to people who live near the factories.

Many businesses use dangerous materials or produce dangerous wastes. Gas stations, dry cleaners, print shops, film developers, hardware stores, greenhouses, funeral parlors, home decorators, farms, and hair styling salons all use chemicals that can harm the environment. Transportation creates large amounts of toxic waste from the oil used in cars and the grease used for brakes in trucks. Even x-ray machines at airports cause toxic waste. These wastes contribute to the huge amount of dangerous substances that threaten us.

We cannot easily give up the toxic products that are necessary to our way of life. For example, batteries are used in cars, trucks, radios, and small toys. These batteries contain **heavy metals,** such as cadmium, mercury, and lead. If batteries are improperly discarded, heavy metals can leak into the soil and pollute the **ground water**.

Many businesses, such as greenhouses, use chemicals that can harm the environment.

These batteries were used in cars and trucks. They contain heavy metals such as cadmium, mercury and lead.

OTHER SOURCES OF TOXIC WASTE

Businesses are not the only sources of toxic waste. Hospitals and doctors' offices also produce dangerous waste. Many of the drugs used to heal people, as well as the mercury used in silver fillings for their teeth, can harm the environment. Substances that can improve health can also kill, especially if people are exposed to them in large quantities. Even the boxes, cans, and bottles in which these drugs are stored are a problem.

X-ray machines and the energy that runs them are also dangerous. Users cannot just toss these items into a trash can and forget them. Medical waste must be carefully disposed of.

Military bases and airports are another source of dangerous materials. High-powered fuels for rockets and planes give off deadly fumes when they are burned. These fuels are toxic wastes that require special handling.

X-ray machines and the energy that runs them can be dangerous. Medical waste must be carefully disposed of.

16

High-powered rocket fuels for military planes give off deadly fumes when they are burned. These fuels are toxic wastes that require special handling.

17

Asbestos, banned in 1986, is a highly toxic substance that was often used in industry, housing and fireproof clothing. It can cause a deadly disease when small bits enter the lungs.

18

FORMS OF TOXIC WASTE

Three forms of toxic wastes affect the environment: solids, liquids, and gases. Toxic solids, in the form of dust and smoke, leave factories and incinerators through smokestacks. These small bits of waste are carried long distances in the air, fog, rain, dew, or snow. They penetrate soil and poison water. If they settle on pasture land, they may enter the bodies of cattle, chickens, or pigs. Such a transfer may poison the meat products we eat or the milk we drink.

One form of harmful solid is **asbestos**, a mineral material which is used in industry, housing, and fireproof clothing. For many years, builders thought asbestos was safe. They used it to insulate homes, electric wires, appliances, garden hoses, and furnaces. Then scientists discovered that asbestos causes a deadly disease when small bits enter the lungs. In 1986, the EPA banned the use of asbestos in most areas of manufacturing.

Liquid wastes also can be toxic. Some very strong solutions, such as cleaning fluid, drain cleaner, sludge from garages, and rust remover, can actually dissolve the containers that hold them. Users and waste handlers have to wear protective clothing and gloves to keep these strong liquids from burning their skin and eyes.

Many toxic wastes may take the form of gases. Some factories produce deadly gases in processes such as dyeing cloth, tanning leather, or bleaching paper. Many machines burn fuels that produce dangerous gases, such as the fumes from welding torches.

These gases can damage the thin air sacs in human lungs. People who use or help dispose of these dangerous gases often wear face masks lined with **activated charcoal** to protect them from breathing toxic fumes.

Some toxic wastes create a foul smell when they are exposed to the air. Others may have no odor at all. One example of a deadly odorless substance is **carbon monoxide**. This gas comes from car exhaust. Odorless toxic wastes are even more dangerous than those that have an odor, because people may not be aware that a toxic waste is present.

Some toxic liquids and solids become deadly gases when they ignite. Fires containing rubber, plastic, and other **synthetic** products may kill anyone who breathes the fumes. For this reason, firefighters breathe air from oxygen tanks when they enter a burning building.

Another result of toxic waste is **smog**. Smog is a mixture of toxic gases and moisture in the air. Smog is most likely to occur in cities where too many cars and trucks crowd the highways. When changes in the atmosphere cause moisture to lie close to the ground, smog becomes thick. It may bother normal breathing and cause eyes to water. When smog reaches dangerous levels, news reporters may warn joggers not to run and children not to play outdoors. They may also suggest that elderly people and people with heart disease or lung

problems remain indoors until the smog disappears.

Wherever smog is found in the world, it is a serious danger. In certain parts of the United States, such as Los Angeles, California, and Denver, Colorado, smog is a common problem that can weaken cloth and rubber, destroy metal, and cause people to cough. In London, England, where people frequently burn coal to heat their homes, smog has become so dangerous that it has killed people. In central Europe, smog has wiped out ancient forests.

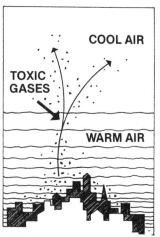

WARM AIR RISES, CARRYING TOXIC GASES UP AND AWAY.

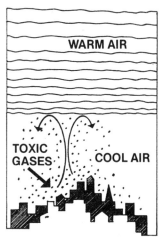

COOL AIR MOVING IN UNDER WARM AIR DOES NOT RISE. THIS TRAPS TOXIC GASES, CREATING SMOG.

Smog is a mixture of toxic gases and moisture in the air.

Firefighters must breathe air from oxygen tanks when entering a burning building. The smoke and fumes can be deadly if inhaled.

Nuclear power plants produce a deadly type of toxic waste called radioactive waste.

RADIOACTIVE WASTES

An even deadlier type of toxic waste is **radioactive** waste. This waste gives off energy in the form of harmful rays or particles. Even the water used to cool engines driven by radioactive fuels can be hazardous. Toxic waste of this type comes from scientific laboratories, hospitals, **nuclear power plants**, and military bases.

Radioactive waste is so toxic that workers usually seal it in lead containers. These containers are carefully marked and buried in deep holes. Some types of radioactive waste must stay buried for up to 10,000 years before they are safe.

Natural disasters such as earthquakes or explosions can cause cracks in these containers. Workers check the containers frequently to be certain that none of the radioactive waste is leaking. If there is a leak, the soil around the container must be removed and buried along with the waste.

Earthquakes are a constant threat when radioactive waste is buried in containers in the earth. Any cracks or leaks in the containers caused by a quake must be corrected immediately.

Polluted ground water can enter the body through swimming at your favorite beach.

CHAPTER THREE

EFFECTS OF TOXIC WASTE

Toxic wastes are dangerous not only to humans, but also to plants and animals. They are a serious health problem that can cause severe illnesses, deformities, and sometimes death. To protect yourself from toxic wastes, you must understand how they enter and affect people, plants, and animals.

HOW TOXIC WASTES AFFECT THE BODY

Toxic wastes enter the body in a variety of ways. Polluted ground water can enter the body through drinking, bathing, swimming, or eating fish or vegetables that absorb wastes. Heavy metals can collect in the body's fatty cells and damage the heart, brain, liver, kidneys, or nerves. The damage, which is slow to make itself known, can lead to nausea, improper growth, numbness, or even death.

Many common products can cause similar harm. For example, bags of fertilizer, fumes from diesel-powered cars and trucks, spot remover, paint thinner, television sets, and ink contain strong chemicals. These chemicals can harm the body in several ways. Some may cause **cancer** or abnormal growth in body cells. Some may affect unborn babies and animals. A third type may change reproductive cells and cause future generations to suffer birth defects.

Toxic waste poisoning can affect every part of the human body. Toxic poisoning can make a person blind, deaf, insane, or unable to fight off disease. Even in small amounts, some toxic wastes burn skin, eyes, and nasal linings, and cause rashes. Other wastes cause kidney failure, asthma, breathing problems, headaches, brain damage, speech defects, and stillbirths. Harmful substances can also create unusual changes in people's behavior. Some symptoms are forgetfulness and the ability to concentrate.

TOXIC WASTES AND NATURE

Toxic wastes affect other living things besides humans. Hazardous substances can burn spots on leaves and twigs. Sometimes they stunt the growth of plants. Other toxic wastes may keep plants from producing flowers or fruit.

Dangerous toxic wastes in streams may cause fish to develop abnormally or grow tumors. Sometimes a large number of fish may die at one time. Such **fish kills** are usually a sign that toxic waste is polluting the waterway.

Other animals affected by toxic waste may leave their normal nesting and feeding areas. They may produce fewer or deformed young. Bird and turtle eggs may have soft shells. These animals cannot survive or reproduce normally if toxic waste harms their environment.

Dangerous toxic wastes in streams can cause fish kills and animals to leave their normal nesting and feeding areas.

Heavy earth-moving equipment is used to pack waste in sanitary landfills.

CHAPTER FOUR

DISPOSING OF TOXIC WASTES

The ideal way to control toxic wastes is to stop creating them. Unfortunately, such a big change is not practical. Although vehicles produce harmful gases, we cannot expect people to give them up to save the environment. Many other products are also helpful, such as the radioactive materials that help us locate and treat disease. Thus, we simply have to find more effective ways to dispose of toxic wastes.

USING THE EARTH

In early times, people dumped their garbage away from where they lived, in gullies, rivers, or the ocean. Today, dumping is not allowed because officials recognize that careless dumping can pollute the environment. The best way to use the earth to dispose of wastes is to create **sanitary landfills**. Such landfills are lined with plastic and clay, then filled with waste. **Sanitation engineers** then layer dirt and clay over toxic wastes and press them down with heavy earth-moving equipment. They cover up the wastes to stop human contact with them.

Unfortunately, sanitary landfills are expensive to operate. Sometimes they are too far away to be useful to most people. When trucks have to travel great distances to landfills, they cause heavy traffic. There is also a danger of accidents or spills along the way. As land becomes more expensive and less usable to an area, city planners often look for other ways to deal with wastes.

Another problem with landfills is that they do not actually get rid of dangerous materials. Deadly substances such as asbestos still exist, even if they are underground. Toxic liquids may still ooze from the waste heaps and pollute the ground water. Some landfills contain special pipe systems to carry away these dangerous liquids and store them more safely.

Landfills may also form dangerous gases, such as **carbon dioxide** and **methane**. When materials begin to decay under the earth, they often form pockets of gas that can start to burn or explode. To release these gases, landfill workers must pipe them away safely. Some systems use the gas as a cheap source of energy, which can light, cool, and heat homes and run factories.

An additional method for disposal of toxic wastes, other than landfills, is to place wastes in sealed steel containers. These containers are then buried in salt beds deep in the earth. Such salt beds exist in desert areas in the western United States, such as near the Yucca Mountains of Nevada.

However, some people disagree with the salt bed method of disposal. They believe that a natural disturbance, such as an earthquake or volcanic explosion, could disturb the salt bed and break open the containers. They fear that the harmful wastes may escape the deep layers of salt.

A similar method of using deep portions of the earth as storage for toxic wastes is to inject the wastes into deep wells. By locating cracks or drilling holes thousands of feet into solid rock, disposal engineers force liquid toxic waste far below the earth's surface. But like the salt bed method of disposal, this system is often questioned. Pollution experts fear that an explosion or shift in underground layers of rock may release the toxic wastes into ground water.

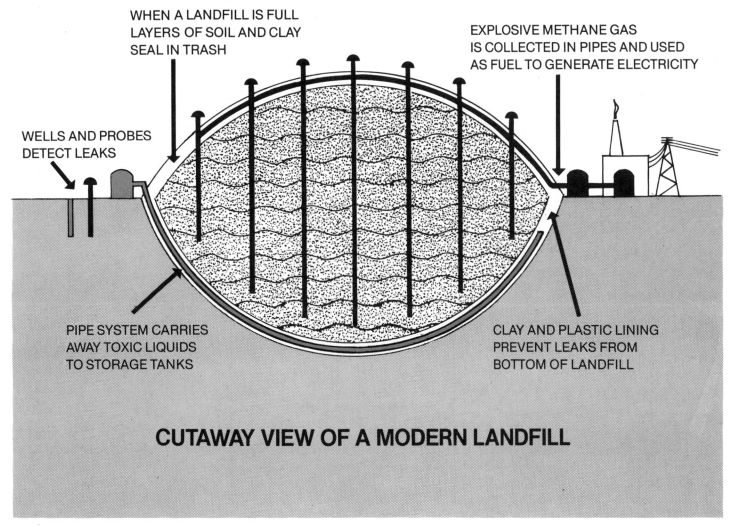

WHEN A LANDFILL IS FULL
LAYERS OF SOIL AND CLAY
SEAL IN TRASH

EXPLOSIVE METHANE GAS
IS COLLECTED IN PIPES AND USED
AS FUEL TO GENERATE ELECTRICITY

WELLS AND PROBES
DETECT LEAKS

PIPE SYSTEM CARRIES
AWAY TOXIC LIQUIDS
TO STORAGE TANKS

CLAY AND PLASTIC LINING
PREVENT LEAKS FROM
BOTTOM OF LANDFILL

CUTAWAY VIEW OF A MODERN LANDFILL

31

Oil spills such as the one in this photo will have to be treated with tiny living organisms that eat the toxic material. As the organisms digest the waste, the toxic material will break down into a less harmful substance.

OTHER METHODS OF DISPOSAL

The question of toxic waste has caused scientists to experiment with many methods of protecting people from toxic materials. In some parts of the United States, large concrete **incinerators** burn dangerous materials. They use coal, oil, and other fuels to burn and reduce the amount of waste. Within the thick walls of the incinerators, waste handlers place waste in a very hot fire. The trash burns quickly to ash.

Even though burning can decrease toxic wastes by about 90%, there are still problems with this method. The remaining dangerous ash, composed mainly of heavy metals, must be disposed of. Also, escaping dust and fumes can pollute the air. To control this problem, smoke is sent up very tall chimneys, where special **stack scrubbers** remove heavy particles to keep the burning waste from harming nearby people and land. Another purpose of scrubbers is to control **acid rain**. This type of moisture forms when harmful waste particles mix with rain or snow and damage the plants and animals it falls on.

A more technical method to decrease the danger of toxic wastes is to remove them from larger bodies of trash. For example, by using a **sedimentation** process, disposal engineers can cause heavy particles to settle to the bottom of a body of trash and leave above a harmless liquid.

A similar method is the use of **evaporation**. Toxic mixtures are heated to change the harmless liquid they contain into gases. The gases vanish into the air, leaving the harmful solids behind.

Another similar method which uses the same principle is **filtration**. By filtering out toxic solids, workers can reduce the size of the toxic waste problem.

Experimental waste treatment processes show promise of decreasing the dangers of toxic waste. Some toxic solids can be made into small pellets. Others are exposed to strong chemicals that remove the danger. A few types of toxic waste, such as oil spills, are exposed to tiny living organisms, particularly algae and bacteria, that eat the toxic materials. As the organisms digest the wastes, the toxic materials break down into less harmful substances.

33

Composting is another process which involves layering earth and living material on top of the toxic waste. This is not the same type of composting that people use at home to reduce grass clippings and kitchen waste into mulch. It is far more complex and uses special living organisms to change toxic waste into a harmless material. If this special compost remains damp, it can soon cause some types of toxic waste to rot. Both of these biological methods are useful, but they require a staff of scientists, and a large amount of space to succeed. Also, they only work for certain kinds of toxic wastes.

An even better solution for toxic waste is recycling. The government is encouraging companies to share toxic wastes which might be useful in some other manufacturing process. By putting the unused materials to work in another form, manufacturers can save the cost and worry of getting rid of them.

Through composting, living organisms are used to change toxic waste into a harmless material.

Biodegradable household products can be purchased to help prevent toxic waste.

Workers must wear single-piece suits and face masks to safely manage toxic wastes.

REMAINING WATCHFUL

Protection of the environment from the effects of toxic waste is a never-ending task. The EPA is the government office responsible for guarding our country from pollution. The EPA tries to protect humans and the environment. This agency keeps a close eye on ash from incinerators that burn toxic waste. The EPA also examines steel drums filled with toxic or radioactive wastes. It measures heavy metals and harmful chemicals in the air and water.

Another important job of the agency is to protect sanitation workers from coming in contact with dangerous wastes. The EPA requires workers to wear ear plugs and goggles for protection. Also, it checks work suits to be sure they are thick enough to keep out harmful liquids and gases. Sometimes single-piece suits are necessary to cover their entire bodies. When workers enter thick clouds of hazardous dust or gas, the EPA requires them to wear face masks. In these ways, workers can safely manage toxic wastes.

The Environmental Protection Agency posts warning signs when toxic substances are present.

37

When gardening, avoid toxic herbicides by using biodegradable or natural products.

CHAPTER FIVE

YOUR PART

People cannot stop making toxic waste. As long as there are homes, farms, hospitals, power plants, airports, and businesses, there will be toxic wastes. However, people can be more aware of the manner in which businesses and institutions dispose of deadly materials. Then people like the Kilbys might not have to leave their homes to avoid contact with toxic wastes.

Also, each person can create less toxic waste and be more careful about disposing of it. Here are some suggestions that anyone can use to help decrease the problem of toxic wastes.

RESTRICT HAZARDOUS WASTE

1. Purchase only nontoxic materials, such as water-based art paint, markers, and other art supplies.

2. Avoid **aerosol** cans and toxic cleaners. Rely on simple cleaning products, such as vinegar and baking soda.
3. Avoid **herbicides** by weeding and mulching to control weeds.
4. Choose water-based housepaints, which are less toxic than those that contain oil.
5. Read labels to be sure that products are not harmful to the environment.
6. Request **biodegradable** or natural products for home and garden use.

HELP KEEP THE ENVIRONMENT CLEAN AND SAFE

1. Dispose of paint, **pesticides**, aerosol cans, batteries, and other toxic wastes safely. Never burn any kind of garbage.
2. Dispose of used oil at a recycling center or at a service station that provides a waste disposal service. Never pour oil or other toxic substances on the ground or down a drain.
3. Place hazardous wastes in sturdy bags or cans with tight-fitting lids. Tie bag tops securely.
4. Dispose of garbage at curbside on collection days. Keep your dog away from garbage so that it will not tear open trash bags or turn over cans.
5. Follow local laws about the use of landfills for disposal of toxic wastes.

Dispose of used motor oil at a service station or recycling center.
Never pour oil on the ground.

HELPFUL HINTS ACCORDING TO EARTH DAY MAGAZINE

EARTH DAY USA

T.M: 1991 Earth Day Int'l.

Some hazardous wastes pose such a threat to the environment and human health that the only safe way to dispose of it is to have it done by your local waste management facility.

The following list will give you an idea of some products that should be disposed of at your city waste facility:

- AUTOMOBILE PAINT
- FLEA POWDER
- HERBICIDES
- OIL-BASED PAINTS
- VEHICLE BRAKE FLUID
- GASOLINE
- INSECTICIDES
- MOTOR OIL

Take extra care with this hazardous waste until you are ready to dispose of it by:

- KEEPING ALL PRODUCTS OUT OF THE REACH OF CHILDREN AND ANIMALS
- KEEPING PRODUCTS AWAY FROM FLAME OR INTENSE HEAT
- MAKE SURE LIDS ARE SEALED TIGHTLY
- MAKE SURE CONTAINERS ARE KEPT DRY TO PREVENT RUSTING OF CONTAINERS

TIPS FOR DISPOSAL:

- NEVER POUR CHEMICALS DOWN A BASEMENT DRAIN
- NEVER MIX CHEMICALS TOGETHER (They can create a deadly gas)
- FLUSH WASTES DURING THE DAY SO THEY DO NOT STAY IN THE PIPES A LONG TIME
- FLUSH WASTES USING A LARGE AMOUNT OF WATER — TRY TO EMPTY WASTES BEFORE TAKING A SHOWER OR RUNNING THE DISHWASHER THAT WAY ENOUGH WATER FLUSHES THE WASTES WITHOUT USING SO MUCH FRESH WATER.

Other hazardous wastes can be flushed down the drain if they can be mixed with water, or when your city sewage system is able to remove the toxins. Some examples of products that can be flushed in small quantities are:

- LOTIONS
- AMMONIA
- DRAIN OPENER
- RUG SHAMPOO
- PERFUMES
- HOUSEHOLD BLEACH
- GLASS CLEANERS

REMEMBER THE EARTH DAY PLEDGE

"MAKE EVERY DAY EARTH DAY"!

PROTECT YOURSELF

1. Store toxic substances, such as kerosene, solvents, and insect repellents, in their original containers. Keep them out of the reach of children.

2. Never reuse containers that have held toxic wastes.

3. Use toxic materials such as paint and spot remover in a well-ventilated area. Read package directions about what to do if you should swallow or breathe dangerous substances. Keep these materials away from heat and flame.

4. Stay away from old barrels or dump sites that might contain toxic wastes.

5. Never mix strong chemicals, such as chlorine bleach and ammonia.

6. Never burn charcoal or operate a gasoline engine in a closed room, such as a garage or basement.

7. If you come in contact with pesticides or herbicides, change your clothes and shoes and wash all exposed parts of your body.

8. Separate home wastes into recyclable material, unusable waste, and toxic waste. Follow local regulations concerning disposal.

9. Buy foods that contain no **additives**. Carefully wash pesticides off fruits and vegetables.

10. Ask questions. Read articles about toxic waste. By learning more, you can be an effective voice against toxic waste.

Observe streams and ponds for signs of pollution.

ENCOURAGE GOVERNMENT OFFICIALS TO TAKE ACTION

1. Write or call local officials or state or national representatives. Encourage them to vote for laws that promote better handling of toxic waste or radioactive waste. Insist on heavy fines to stop illegal dumping of toxic waste.
2. Support citizen's groups that seek to restrict the dumping or careless burning of toxic materials.
3. Observe streams and ponds near your home. Report unusual changes, such as fish kills, dumping, floating trash, oilslicks, or foul smells.
4. Organize a letter-writing campaign to encourage officials to protect citizens from toxic waste.

ENCOURAGE INDUSTRY TO RECYCLE

1. Buy products from companies that try to control toxic wastes.
2. Write thank-you notes to these companies.

GLOSSARY

acid rain (A syd RAYN)　moisture that mixes with pollution in the air and falls to the earth as rain or snow

activated charcoal (AK tih vay tihd CHAHR kohl)　carbon grains that filter impurities from the air

additives (AD ih tihvz)　chemicals added to foods to keep them fresh or to change their color, smell, or taste

aerosol (AYR uh sahl)　a liquid sprayed from a can containing pressurized gas

asbestos (as BEHS tohs)　a mineral material that is used in insulation and fireproofing

biodegradable (by oh dih GRAYD uh buhl)　capable of breaking down into harmless by-products

by-products (BY prahd uhkts)　waste products made by a factory while it is creating useful goods

cancer (KAN suhr)　an abnormal growth of human tissue that may spread and destroy surrounding tissue

carbon dioxide (KAHR buhn dy AHK syd)　an odorless gas given off by living matter when it decays

carbon monoxide (KAHR buhn muhn AHK syd)   a deadly, odorless gas that results from the burning of gasoline

composting (KAHM pohst ihng)   encouraging the decay of plant material

environment (ihn VYRN mihnt)   the surroundings and influences in which any living thing lives, grows, or develops

Environmental Protection Agency (EPA)   a government office responsible for guarding our environment

evaporation (ee vap uh RAY shuhn)   the change of a liquid into a gas

filtration (fihl TRAY shuhn)   the use of a strainer to separate a solid from a liquid

fish kills (FIHSH KIHLZ)   the death of great numbers of fish due to a change in the environment

ground water (GROWND wat uhr)   water that collects below the earth's surface and feeds wells and springs

heavy metals (HEHV ee MEHT uhlz)   metals, including zinc, mercury, lead, chromium, and arsenic, which can poison humans and animals

herbicides (UHRB ih sydz)   chemicals that kill weeds

incinerators (ihn SIHN uh ray tuhrz)   furnaces with heavy walls that burn wastes safely

landfills (LAND fihlz)   places where wastes are buried safely between layers of earth

methane (MEHTH ayn)   an odorless gas that results from the decay of once-living things

nuclear power plants (NOO klee uhr POW uhr PLANTS) factories that make power by releasing energy from tiny particles

pesticides (PEHST ih sydz)   chemicals that kill unwanted insects, plants, and fungus

polluted (puh LOO tihd)   dirtied or contaminated

radioactive (ray dee oh AK tihv)   giving off harmful particles or rays

recycle (ree SY kuhl)   reuse a discarded item

recycling bins (ree SY klihng BIHNZ)   large containers that store glass, plastic, newspaper, or aluminum cans for collection and reuse

sanitary landfills (SAN ih tar ee LAND fihlz)   a clay-lined pit where garbage is safely buried away from water supplies

sanitation engineers (san ih TAY shuhn ihn jih NEERZ)   see *sanitation workers*

sanitation workers (san ih TAY shuhn WUHRK uhrz)   a public employee who promotes good health by maintaining clean conditions and preventing disease.

sedimentation (sehd ih mihn TAY shuhn)   a method of separation which causes heavy particles to sink to the bottom of a liquid

slag (SLAG)   waste left over from mining operations

smog (SMAHG)   a mixture of hazardous gases with any precipitation, including rain, snow, sleet, and dew

solvents (SAHL vihntz)   a liquid that dissolves a solid material

stack scrubbers (STAK SKRUHB uhrz)   devices in smokestacks that remove bits of heavy metals and other particles from the fumes that escape

synthetic (sihn THEHT ihk)   manufactured or artificial

toxic wastes (TAHK sihk WAYSTS)   any kind of waste that can can poison living things